Wonderful World of Colors

COLORFUL RACE CARS

Rebecca Izumo

HABA®

PowerKiDS
press™

NEW YORK

Published in 2018 by The Rosen Publishing Group, Inc.
29 East 21st Street, New York, NY 10010

First Edition

Editor: Elizabeth Krajnik
Book Design: Michael Flynn
Interior Layout: Rachel Rising

Photo Credits: Cover © iStock.com/Henrik5000; pp. 5, 24 Natursports/Shutterstock.com; p. 6 ZRyzner/Shutterstock.com; p. 9,10,13 David Acosta Allely/Shutterstock.com; p. 14 TFoxFoto/Shutterstock.com; pp. 17, 24 Yuriy Ponomarev/Shutterstock.com; p. 18 © iStock.com/BanksPhotos; pp. 21 Monika Wisniewska/Shutterstock.com; pp. 22, 24 Jon Feingersh/Getty.

Cataloging-in-Publication Data

Names: Izumo, Rebecca.
Title: Colorful race cars / Rebecca Izumo.
Description: New York : PowerKids Press, 2018. | Series: Wonderful world of colors | Includes index.
Identifiers: ISBN 9781538320952 (pbk.) | ISBN 9781538320969 (library bound) | ISBN 9781508161691 (6 pack)
Subjects: LCSH: Automobiles, Racing–Juvenile literature. | Colors–Juvenile literature.
Classification: LCC TL236.I98 2018 | DDC 629.228–dc23

Manufactured in China

CPSIA Compliance Information: Batch #BS17PK: For Further Information contact Rosen Publishing, New York, New York at 1-800-237-9932

Please visit: www.rosenpublishing.com and www.habausa.com

CONTENTS

Fast and Slow

Drivers race cars around a racetrack.

Some cars go fast. Some cars go slow.

Fans watch the race.

The Red Car Is Fast

There's a red car, a blue car, and a green car. The red car goes fast. It zooms around the track! The driver is in first place!

The red car is in the lead. The blue car is in second place. This car does not go as fast as the red car.

Now the blue car and the red car are tied.

The blue car goes faster than the red car.

The blue car is in the lead!

The green car is in last place. If the green car goes slow it won't win the race. Can the green car go faster?

13

Flags at the Race Track

We see flags at the racetrack. The flags tell drivers what to do. Each flag means something different.

The yellow flag means slow down. The drivers slow down during an accident. The yellow flag keeps the drivers safe.

17

18

The green flag means go fast. Drivers need to go fast to win the race. The green flag also means it's safe to drive fast again after an accident.

The checkered flag is special. It means that a driver has won the race. The winning car has crossed the finish line.

21

Who will win the race? The red car passes the blue car. The red car is in the lead. The blue car is in second place. The green car is in last place. The red car is the fastest. The red car wins!

WORDS TO KNOW

driver

flag

track

INDEX